"This series is a tremendous resource for those wanting to study and teach the Bible with an understanding of how the gospel is woven throughout Scripture. Here are gospel-minded pastors and scholars doing gospel business from all the Scriptures. This is a biblical and theological feast preparing God's people to apply the entire Bible to all of life with heart and mind wholly committed to Christ's priorities."

BRYAN CHAPELL, President Emeritus, Covenant Theological Seminary; Senior Pastor, Grace Presbyterian Church, Peoria, Illinois

"Mark Twain may have smiled when he wrote to a friend, 'I didn't have time to write you a short letter, so I wrote you a long letter.' But the truth of Twain's remark remains serious and universal, because well-reasoned, compact writing requires extra time and extra hard work. And this is what we have in the Crossway Bible study series *Knowing the Bible*. The skilled authors and notable editors provide the contours of each book of the Bible as well as the grand theological themes that bind them together as one Book. Here, in a 12-week format, are carefully wrought studies that will ignite the mind and the heart."

R. KENT HUGHES, Visiting Professor of Practical Theology, Westminster Theological Seminary

"*Knowing the Bible* brings together a gifted team of Bible teachers to produce a high-quality series of study guides. The coordinated focus of these materials is unique: biblical content, provocative questions, systematic theology, practical application, and the gospel story of God's grace presented all the way through Scripture."

PHILIP G. RYKEN, President, Wheaton College

"These *Knowing the Bible* volumes provide a significant and very welcome variation on the general run of inductive Bible studies. This series provides substantial instruction, as well as teaching through the very questions that are asked. *Knowing the Bible* then goes even further by showing how any given text links with the gospel, the whole Bible, and the formation of theology. I heartily endorse this orientation of individual books to the whole Bible and the gospel, and I applaud the demonstration that sound theology was not something invented later by Christians, but is right there in the pages of Scripture."

GRAEME L. GOLDSWORTHY, former lecturer, Moore Theological College; author, *According to Plan*, *Gospel and Kingdom*, *The Gospel in Revelation*, and *Gospel and Wisdom*

"What a gift to earnest, Bible-loving, Bible-searching believers! The organization and structure of the Bible study format presented through the *Knowing the Bible* series is so well conceived. Students of the Word are led to understand the content of passages through perceptive, guided questions, and they are given rich insights and application all along the way in the brief but illuminating sections that conclude each study. What potential growth in depth and breadth of understanding these studies offer! One can only pray that vast numbers of believers will discover more of God and the beauty of his Word through these rich studies."

BRUCE A. WARE, Professor of Christian Theology, The Southern Baptist Theological Seminary

KNOWING THE BIBLE

J. I. Packer, Theological Editor
Dane C. Ortlund, Series Editor
Lane T. Dennis, Executive Editor

•   •   •   •   •   •

Genesis	Psalms	Jonah, Micah, and Nahum	Ephesians
Exodus	Proverbs	Nahum	Philippians
Leviticus	Ecclesiastes	Haggai, Zechariah, and Malachi	Colossians and Philemon
Numbers	Song of Solomon	and Malachi	Philemon
Deuteronomy	Isaiah	Matthew	1–2 Thessalonians
Joshua	Jeremiah	Mark	1–2 Timothy and
Judges	Lamentations,	Luke	Titus
Ruth and Esther	Habakkuk, and	John	Hebrews
1–2 Samuel	Zephaniah	Acts	James
1–2 Kings	Ezekiel	Romans	1–2 Peter and Jude
1–2 Chronicles	Daniel	1 Corinthians	1–3 John
Ezra and Nehemiah	Hosea	2 Corinthians	Revelation
Job	Joel, Amos, and Obadiah	Galatians	

•   •   •   •   •   •

J. I. PACKER is Board of Governors' Professor of Theology at Regent College (Vancouver, BC). Dr. Packer earned his DPhil at the University of Oxford. He is known and loved worldwide as the author of the best-selling book *Knowing God*, as well as many other titles on theology and the Christian life. He serves as the General Editor of the ESV Bible and as the Theological Editor for the *ESV Study Bible*.

LANE T. DENNIS is President of Crossway, a not-for-profit publishing ministry. Dr. Dennis earned his PhD from Northwestern University. He is Chair of the ESV Bible Translation Oversight Committee and Executive Editor of the *ESV Study Bible*.

DANE C. ORTLUND is Executive Vice President of Bible Publishing and Bible Publisher at Crossway. He is a graduate of Covenant Theological Seminary (MDiv, ThM) and Wheaton College (BA, PhD). Dr. Ortlund has authored several books and scholarly articles in the areas of Bible, theology, and Christian living.

SONG OF SOLOMON

A 12-WEEK STUDY

Jay Harvey

CROSSWAY®

WHEATON, ILLINOIS

Crossway is a publishing ministry of Good News Publishers.

VP			27	26	25	24	23	22	21	20	19	18
15	14	13	12	11	10	9	8	7	6	5	4	3	2	1

TABLE OF CONTENTS

▲

SERIES PREFACE

KNOWING THE BIBLE, as the series title indicates, was created to help readers know and understand the meaning, the message, and the God of the Bible. Each volume in the series consists of 12 units that progressively take the reader through a clear, concise study of one or more books of the Bible. In this way, any given volume can fruitfully be used in a 12-week format either in group study, such as in a church-based context, or in individual study. Of course, these 12 studies could be completed in fewer or more than 12 weeks, as convenient, depending on the context in which they are used.

Each study unit gives an overview of the text at hand before digging into it with a series of questions for reflection or discussion. The unit then concludes by highlighting the gospel of grace in each passage ("Gospel Glimpses"), identifying whole-Bible themes that occur in the passage ("Whole-Bible Connections"), and pinpointing Christian doctrines that are affirmed in the passage ("Theological Soundings").

The final component to each unit is a section for reflecting on personal and practical implications from the passage at hand. The layout provides space for recording responses to the questions proposed, and we think readers need to do this to get the full benefit of the exercise. The series also includes definitions of key words. These definitions are indicated by a note number in the text and are found at the end of each chapter.

Lastly, to help understand the Bible in this deeper way, we urge readers to use the ESV Bible and the *ESV Study Bible*, which are available in various print and digital formats, including online editions at esv.org. The *Knowing the Bible* series is also available online.

May the Lord greatly bless your study as you seek to know him through knowing his Word.

J. I. Packer
Lane T. Dennis

WEEK 1: OVERVIEW

▲

The Song of Solomon is a love poem that celebrates the love between a woman and a man both before and after they are married. The Song of Solomon is part of the biblical genre of wisdom literature. In wisdom literature, God provides divine perspective concerning the good and righteous life. In the Song of Solomon, the reader encounters a divine perspective on human love. We see in this song an ideal of human love displayed between a young woman and a young man. We see them before their wedding as they anticipate the day in which their love will find expression in sexual union. We also see them after their wedding, dealing with the insecurities and challenges that come in even the best of marriages. The Song of Solomon is a rich and vivid account of human love, an account that is desperately needed in our own time. So much confusion about love and sexuality persists in our culture. Here God provides clarity that leads to greater holiness, joy, and fulfillment.

This poem is called the Song of Solomon because it was either written by or dedicated to Solomon. Solomon is not the groom in the poem but rather seems to appear more as a negative counterexample. This poem shows that two ordinary people can enjoy the extraordinary blessings of marriage and, in this way, surpass the earthly glories of King Solomon. Solomon had great riches but also many wives and concubines. Thus he is not a good example of God's design for marriage, in which one man and one woman are to commit to each other for a lifetime. Does this mean that Solomon could not have written the book? No; it may be that Solomon wrote the Song of Solomon toward the end of his life when he had repented of the lifestyle that so characterized his reign. In this sense, the Song of Solomon could be the wisdom that comes from repentance: Solomon is seeking to persuade and instruct the reader to live more wisely and righteously than he did.

(Readers should note that the subheadings in ESV Bibles identify Solomon as the bridegroom. For a thorough discussion of this and other views, see the *ESV Study Bible*.)

Because of its romantic content and vivid imagery, the Song of Solomon has often been seen as appropriate for those entering or enjoying marriage, but not for wider study. However, as part of the canon of inspired Scriptures, this book is given "for teaching, for reproof, for correction, and for training in righteousness" (2 Tim. 3:16). In the Song of Solomon, readers catch a glimpse of the joy and dangers of romantic life and sexual intimacy while being spared from the pains that come with sexual experimentation. In so doing, readers are likewise being equipped to be faithful spouses relationally and sexually. Even for those who have experienced sexual woundedness or brokenness, the Song of Solomon may provide additional insight that can aid healing. For those who are called to singleness (whether by conviction or by providence), the Song of Solomon can also point to Christ. Indeed, the marriage put on display in this book is intended ultimately to point all readers to Christ's love for his bride, the church[1]: "'... a man shall leave his father and mother and hold fast to his wife, and the two shall become one flesh.' This mystery is profound, and I am saying that it refers to Christ and the church" (Eph. 5:31–32). Thus, regardless of one's station in life, the Song of Solomon is intended to minister to each reader as the very Word of God.

▶ Placing the Song of Solomon in the Larger Story

The Bible begins with the creation of the heavens and the earth. Adam and Eve are the capstone of creation. To this first couple God gives the mandate to subdue the earth to his glory. He also instructs them to be fruitful and multiply. The first indication of the significance of marriage is seen in how it is the God-ordained institution to fill the earth with his glory. Sexual intimacy is an integral part of this institution, providing powerful pleasure for procreation and as a means of strengthening and nurturing the marriage bond. As the biblical narrative unfolds, however, we see an even greater purpose for marriage. The love a man has for a woman is patterned after the greater love that Christ has for the church—a love that led him to give himself for her. In the Song of Solomon, we see a righteous expression of human love and sexuality. The Song thus functions at two levels: as a guide to the purposes of marriage instituted at Eden, and as a poetic metaphor for Christ's love for the church. As a metaphor, however, its details are not to be pressed for doctrinal precision.

The fall[2] of the human race is also a part of the biblical story. The first couple sinned and came under the judgment of God. As a result, the sexual dimension of the human race is fallen, as seen in the many sinful expressions of sexuality prevalent today. As a reaction to the pervasive presence of sexual sin, some in the history of the church have drifted to the unbiblical position that all human sexual desire is sinful. The Song of Solomon reminds us, however, that it is by God's good design that the love between a man and a woman finds elaborate verbal and sexual expression. Indeed, the Song celebrates the physical dimension of human love. This portion of God's Word should be studied and read today because it brings clarity and balance to a church living in a sexually confused world. Avoiding this book creates a void of teaching about human sexuality, a void that will be easily filled by the culture.

Additionally, the Song of Solomon can teach us about our relationship with Christ. Jesus declares in John's Gospel, "I am the good shepherd. I know my own and my own know me, just as the Father knows me and I know the Father; and I lay down my life for the sheep" (John 10:14–15). Insofar as the Song of Solomon presents an ideal love of the shepherd for his bride, we can rightly draw inferences about the Good Shepherd's love for his bride. Likewise, we can draw insight from the shepherdess's love of the shepherd for our love of *our* Shepherd. Reading the Song of Solomon in this manner requires us to give full attention first to the Song as a divinely inspired love poem, which will allow us then to seek insight rightly into what analogy[3] may exist for the church's relationship to Christ or the dependence of individual believers upon and love for Jesus, the Great Shepherd of the sheep.

This way of reading the Song of Solomon models for us the way that married couples should think about their own relationship. Every dimension of marriage, including the sexual dimension, provides an opportunity to glorify God. When spouses make the glory of God in Christ the ultimate aim of their marriage, they often discover that the other benefits of marriage are found along the way. On the other hand, when the benefits of marriage—companionship, sexual intimacy, children, family stability—are sought apart from the glory of God in Christ, the painful frustration of living in a fallen world can quickly overwhelm the benefits of marriage. The interpretive view of the Song of Solomon taken in this study is both reflected in and shaped by the excellent commentary by Iain Duguid, *Song of Songs: An Introduction and Commentary* (IVP Academic, 2015).

Look up the following verses and write down what they contribute to the Bible's teaching on sexual intimacy:

Genesis 1:26–28

Genesis 2:23–25

Proverbs 5:15–23

1 Corinthians 7:2–5

Ephesians 5:28–33

Hebrews 13:4

Revelation 21:1–2

Key Verse

"I adjure you, O daughters of Jerusalem, by the gazelles or the does of the field, that you not stir up or awaken love until it pleases." (Song 2:7; compare 3:5; 8:4)

Date and Historical Background

The first verse of the Song reads, "The Song of Songs, which is Solomon's." This could mean that Solomon wrote the Song himself or that it was written in his honor or memory, or even under his oversight. Solomon appears in the Song only as a contrastive figure, with no direct speech. In our reading, his role is primarily a negative one in the Song. His experience with many women serves as a superficial foil for the pure and exclusive love between the ordinary man and woman in the poem. As poetic wisdom literature, the Song's date and occasion are not as central to its interpretation as are its own content and structure. (See page 1211 in the *ESV Study Bible* for an extended discussion of date and background.)

Outline and Structure

I. Title (1:1)

II. Prologue (1:2–2:7)

III. Before the Wedding: Joined and Separated (2:8–3:5)

IV. The Wedding (3:6–5:1)

V. After the Wedding: Separated and Rejoined (5:2–6:3)

VI. Contemplation and Renewed Consummation (6:4–8:4)

VII. Epilogue (8:5–14)

As You Get Started

What is the most challenging aspect of the Bible's teaching on marriage and sexuality for you from the passages explored above?

Review the outline of the Song of Solomon in this guide. Which sections are most intriguing to you, and why?

Is it surprising to you that God has provided in Scripture such a positive and rich account of human sexuality? If so, why? How do you hope to grow in your relationship with Christ as a result of this study?

As You Finish This Unit . . .

Pray for God to grow your faith through this study and to allow you to apply the wisdom that you gain about biblical sexuality to his glory, your own purity, and the good of those whom God has placed in your life.

Definitions

[1] **Church** – From a Greek word meaning "assembly." The body of believers in Jesus Christ, referring either to all believers everywhere or to a local gathering of believers.

[2] **The fall** – Adam and Eve's disobeying of God by eating the fruit from the tree of the knowledge of good and evil, resulting in their loss of innocence and favor with God and the introduction of sin and its effects into the world (Genesis 3; Rom. 5:12–21; 1 Cor. 15:21–22).

[3] **Analogy** – A form of reasoning in which one thing is considered similar to another in a certain respect. An example is Jesus' comparison of his approaching death and burial with Jonah's time inside a great fish (Matt. 12:40).

Week 2: The Desire of the Woman

Song of Solomon 1:1–4

The Place of the Passage

A unique feature of the Song that readers should appreciate is how the voice of the woman is given the place of greatest prominence. These first verses make it clear that what follows will be a dynamic and powerful expression of human love. We might say that the Song of Solomon begins with strong statements of the woman's desire for her future spouse.

The Big Picture

The woman expresses her longing for the physical affection of her beloved.

> ### Reflection and Discussion

Read through the complete passage for this study, Song of Solomon 1:1–4. Then read the passages and related questions below and record your responses.

The Song is the "song of songs" in the sense that it is the ultimate song. Why is it fitting to describe a song about human love as the ultimate of all songs?

The woman makes two bold requests in these verses. What are they? (Hint: one is stated as a general wish and the other as a direct command.)

The woman exclaims, "The king has brought me into his chambers" (v. 4). This is a metaphor[1]; the woman is speaking of her beloved, but as she yearns for his affection, she describes him as a king. The woman also says that the name of her beloved is like "oil poured out," most likely a reference to his reputation. From her point of view, what do these metaphors suggest with regard to the relationship between character and reputation and her physical desire for her beloved?

The latter half of verse 4 is the first of seven instances in which we hear from the woman's friends. These friends are generally a positive support for the woman throughout the Song. What is their assessment of her future groom?

It is a reality that when we enter into a relationship, we will encounter the opinions of others about our chosen spouse. What role ought such opinions play in our choice of a spouse?

Read through the following three sections on *Gospel Glimpses*, *Whole-Bible Connections*, and *Theological Soundings*. Then take time to consider the *Personal Implications* these sections may have for you.

Gospel Glimpses

FREEDOM IN CHRIST. The woman is bold in her expression of sexual desire for her beloved. These desires are given by God for the blessing of his people. While they are easily distorted, there is a time for such desires to be unleashed with full enthusiasm. Believers in Christ can freely embrace the gift of sexual intimacy in the context of marriage. This may require seeking forgiveness and healing from past sins, and may also require cultivation of trust and freedom within a newly formed marriage. But from the start, the Song of Solomon shows us that we can be confident of God's blessing in Christ on such expressions of love for one's spouse.

Whole-Bible Connections

MALE AND FEMALE COMPLEMENTARITY. The Song of Solomon follows the biblical pattern set forth in Genesis, in which sexual fulfillment is to be found between male and female, bound together in the context of marriage. This understanding is vital for biblical sexual ethics.[2] The shepherdess in the Song is expressing her desire for her beloved, a male shepherd. The Genesis account makes clear that the female sex was created to be (literally) "like opposite" her male counterpart (see Gen. 2:18 and the notes in the *ESV Study Bible*). The woman is like the man in many ways, but she is also opposite, or corresponding to, the man in some obvious ways. This complementarity is the basis for the intimacy of sexual union.

MARRIAGE AS A TEMPORARY INSTITUTION. The Song of Solomon clearly presents sexual intimacy in marriage as a good gift of God. However, we must also note that sexual intimacy is not to be seen as an essential aspect of human experience. Many married couples will go through seasons without sexual intimacy. Other men and women will be called to a life of singleness, in which sexual intimacy is not possible. In fact, one day sexual intimacy will cease for all people when Christ returns to consummate[3] the work of his kingdom (Matt. 22:30). At that point, the mystery of the union of Christ and the church (marriage) will give way to the reality of Christ's union with the church in a new heavens and a new earth. This progression of the history of salvation[4] cautions us against exalting marriage and sexual intimacy to the position of ultimacy in the human experience.

Theological Soundings

THE BEAUTY OF HUMAN LANGUAGE. The Song of Solomon uses figurative language. When the woman calls her beloved a "king" and asks him to draw her into his chambers, she is speaking metaphorically. To her, he is a king. To her, his bedroom is like the chambers of a great king. This type of language permeates the Song of Solomon. As creatures made in the image of God, human beings are able to employ language in poetic and abstract ways in order to capture greater depths of feelings and emotion. This type of artistry of expression in oral and written language ought to be cultivated and employed.

THE FEMALE VOICE. Modern readers may be surprised to see the Bible giving full place to a woman's expression of her physical desires for her beloved. Although there are aspects of traditional cultures (both Western and non-Western) that downplay or diminish the presence or appropriateness of female sexual desire, the Song of Solomon stands against such biases. Like the Song of Solomon, the apostle Paul also affirms the goodness of female sexual desire when he says that "the husband should give to his wife her conjugal rights" (1 Cor.

7:3). In an age of sexual confusion, it is important that we do not downplay the goodness of sex as created by God nor adopt stereotypes of one kind or another regarding the sexual desire of men and women.

Personal Implications

Take time to reflect on the implications of Song of Solomon 1:1–4 for your own life today. Consider what you have learned that might lead you to praise God, repent of sin, and trust in his gracious promises. Write down your reflections under the three headings we have considered and on the passage as a whole.

1. Gospel Glimpses

2. Whole-Bible Connections

3. Theological Soundings

4. Song of Solomon 1:1–4

> ## As You Finish This Unit . . .

Take a moment now to ask for the Lord's blessing and help as you continue in this study of Song of Solomon. And take a moment also to look back through this unit of study, to reflect on some key things that the Lord may be teaching you.

Definitions

[1] **Metaphor** – A figure of speech that draws an analogy between two objects by equating them, even though they are not actually the same thing. An example is Psalm 119:105: "Your word is a lamp to my feet and a light to my path."

[2] **Ethics** – In Christian theology, the study of morality, justice, and virtue in light of the Bible's teachings.

[3] **Consummation** – In Christian theology, the final and full establishment of the kingdom of God, when the heavens and the earth will be made new and God will rule over all things forever (2 Pet. 3:13; Revelation 21–22).

[4] **History of salvation** – God's unified plan for all of history, to accomplish the salvation of his people. He accomplished this salvation plan in the work of Jesus Christ on earth by his life, crucifixion, burial, and resurrection (Eph. 1:10–12). The consummation of God's plan will take place when Jesus Christ comes again to establish the "new heavens and a new earth in which righteousness dwells" (2 Pet. 3:13).

WEEK 3: THE RESTORATION OF HONOR

Song of Solomon 1:5–11

> ### The Place of the Passage

This passage shows the power of the marriage relationship to restore the honor of one who has felt the sting of life in a fallen world (as each one of us has felt). The words of this passage are words of *vulnerability* on the part of the woman (as opposed to her expressions of desire in 1:2–4) and of *affirmation* on the part of her beloved. We noted in Week 1 that the Song exhibits a general progression in the relationship between the woman and her beloved. The exchange in this week's lesson is a fitting step in this progression, as it reveals the woman's challenging background. She did not enjoy an ideal upbringing, and she shows great vulnerability here. Her beloved does not disappoint us with his response, however. He verbally affirms her in a way appropriate for one who plans to give himself to her in a lifelong covenant of marriage.

> ### The Big Picture

The woman shows vulnerability concerning her physical appearance, and her beloved responds with great affirmation.

> ## Reflection and Discussion

Read through the complete passage for this study, Song of Solomon 1:5–11. Then read the passages and related questions below and record your responses.

In verses 5–6 we learn that the woman is dark from working in the sun. While today it may be fashionable to have tanned skin, in the ancient world this was a sign that one was a laborer. This heroine is not a dainty girl sheltered from the hard knocks of life. She says that she is dark "because the sun has looked upon me" and "my mother's sons were angry with me" (v. 6). She speaks of her body as a (figurative) vineyard, noting that her brothers made her keep a (literal) vineyard such that she did not have time to care for herself. Verse 8 implies that she is currently working as a shepherdess, tending to a flock; this too is hard work. Thus we see that this beautiful picture of marital love is not reserved for the elite but is open to regular people, even those who have had challenging backgrounds or who work in difficult situations. What similar situations of vulnerability or societal challenge can you imagine for a woman considering marriage today?

In verse 8, we see that the man is also a shepherd. How does he respond to the shepherdess's comments about her appearance? How does his response reveal his location?

Many modern women may not appreciate being compared to a "mare among Pharaoh's chariots" (v. 9), but the man is making the point that she is highly esteemed in his eyes. He encourages her by observing, with admiration, that her "cheeks are lovely with ornaments" and her "neck with strings of jewels" (v. 10). If the Song of Solomon is an ideal expression of human love in marriage, what does the man's answer to the woman's expression of vulnerability suggest about God's intention for dialogue in the marriage relationship?

Drawing upon the text, compare and contrast the woman's brothers with her beloved and her chorus of friends as you see them presented in verses 6–11.

Read through the following three sections on *Gospel Glimpses*, *Whole-Bible Connections*, and *Theological Soundings*. Then take time to consider the *Personal Implications* these sections may have for you.

Gospel Glimpses

HUSBANDS, LOVE YOUR WIVES. The woman's beloved speaks words to her that build her up in areas of vulnerability. This is an important aspect of husbands loving their wives as Christ loved the church. In order to do this, men must be secure in Christ themselves so that they are not tempted to be critical of their wives or others in order to build themselves up. Paul makes this connection in Ephesians 5:28–29: "Husbands should love their wives as their own bodies. He who loves his wife loves himself. For no one ever hated his own flesh, but nourishes and cherishes it, just as Christ does the church." The man who has experienced the love and grace of God in Christ is the one who will be most free to nourish and cherish his spouse.

Whole-Bible Connections

MALE HEADSHIP. In Ephesians 5:23 we read, "The husband is the head of the wife even as Christ is the head of the church, his body, and is himself its Savior." Many discussions of male headship revolve around how much and what kind of authority a husband has over his wife. However, in the Song of Solomon the dimension of protection is in the foreground instead. The woman's brothers neglected her and forced her to work the family vineyard to the neglect of her own vineyard, her body. But her beloved will cherish her. The shepherd will become the most important man in her life (replacing her brothers in the text), and he will make her the most important woman in his life (see Gen. 2:24). The priority she holds in his life is matched by his romantic exclamation that she is the "most beautiful among women" (Song 1:8).

Theological Soundings

THE POWER OF WORDS. Human beings are created in the image of God. As image-bearers of God, our words have great power. God's word is so powerful that he can create simply by speaking. As the apostle Paul says in 2 Corinthians 4:6, "God, who said, 'Let light shine out of darkness,' has shone in our hearts to give the light of the knowledge of the glory of God in the face of Jesus Christ." Our words are not powerful enough to create light from darkness, or to cause someone to be born again into a relationship with Jesus Christ. But our words have the power to build up or to tear down. We see the power of words in every area of life, and especially in our most intimate relationships. Spouses know each other's vulnerabilities. Therefore, spouses are in a unique position to speak words well suited to affirm and build up their spouse.

Personal Implications

Take time to reflect on the implications of Song of Solomon 1:5–11 for your own life today. Consider what you have learned that might lead you to praise God, repent of sin, and trust in his gracious promises. Write down your reflections under the three headings we have considered and on the passage as a whole.

1. Gospel Glimpses

2. Whole-Bible Connections

3. Theological Soundings

4. Song of Solomon 1:5–11

> ## As You Finish This Unit . . .

Take a moment now to ask for the Lord's blessing and help as you continue in this study of Song of Solomon. And take a moment also to look back through this unit of study, to reflect on some key things that the Lord may be teaching you.

WEEK 4: ANTICIPATING MARRIAGE

Song of Solomon 1:12–2:7

The Place of the Passage

This passage demonstrates the progression of the relationship between the main characters of the Song. In last week's study, the woman tested the waters of her beloved's affection when she lamented her complexion darkened by years of labor under the sun. His response was effusive in his affirmation of her beauty and his delight in her. Under the safety of his affirmation, her expressions toward her beloved now intensify. This passage contains some of the most sensual and suggestive metaphors in the Song of Solomon.

The Big Picture

The woman and her beloved exchange intimate words affirming their attraction for each other and anticipating their sexual union in marriage.

Reflection and Discussion

Read through the complete passage for this study, Song of Solomon 1:12–2:7. Then read the passages and related questions below and record your responses.

Consider the structure of this passage. In 1:12–14, the woman is musing about her beloved, and then 1:15–2:2 contains a delightful exchange between the two. Finally, in 2:3–7 the Song drifts back to the woman's perspective. The Song is poetry and thus is best appreciated through careful contemplation of its metaphors. List all of the adjectives, descriptive phrases, and metaphors that the woman uses to describe her beloved in 1:12–2:7.

The "beloved" does not refer to the woman by this same term. This is significant, as scholars note, because it suggests again the complementarity of male and female presented in the Song. He refers to her repeatedly as "my love" (1:9, 15; 2:2, 10, 13; 4:1, 7; 5:2; 6:4). In verse 15 the man twice calls the woman beautiful and then says that her "eyes are doves." The eyes are the gateway to the soul; what might it suggest that the man links the woman's beauty with her eyes in verse 15?

In these verses the couple imagines their future together. There remains distance between them: the king is on his couch, but the woman is not with him. Rather, her fragrance wafts over to him and gets his attention (1:12). He responds to her words of affection with his own declaration of affection for her (1:15). In verses 16–17 the woman muses about their future home together; note the shift from "his couch" in verse 12 to "our couch" in verse 16. Their marriage bed is "green," likely in the sense of being fertile and producing children. As poetry, what else does verse 17 suggest about their future life and home as a couple?

Reread verses 2:1–2, another exchange revolving around the woman's insecurity over her appearance. The "rose of Sharon" is actually a common flower (see ESV footnote), not an ornate rose in the modern sense. In other words, the woman complains that she is common. Her beloved turns the image around, however, by placing this common flower in the midst of a bramble, or thorny bush, thereby making it clear that she remains the most attractive compared to all who surround her. While it is important to avoid stereotypes, what does this repeated emphasis on the woman's feelings of insecurity suggest?

Verses 2:3–6 are among the most sensual verses in the Song of Solomon. How does verse 3 suggest that the woman believes that only her betrothed can satisfy her desires?

Some see a reference to sexual intimacy in verse 3, especially given that apple trees were associated with sexuality in the ancient Near East. However, the blessing of shade may also reach back to an earlier motif of protection. How might 1:6 inform one's reading of 2:3?

In 2:6 the woman longs for physical consummation with her beloved. She is "sick with love" (2:5). Her affection for her beloved has risen to a fever pitch. What implications does the advice she offers in 2:7 have for relationships with the opposite sex?

Read through the following three sections on *Gospel Glimpses*, *Whole-Bible Connections*, and *Theological Soundings*. Then take time to consider the *Personal Implications* these sections may have for you.

Gospel Glimpses

WASHED, SANCTIFIED, AND JUSTIFIED. The Song of Solomon presents an ideal picture of human love and sexual intimacy fulfilled in the context of marriage. The woman warns her friends—and us—not to awaken desires for such intimacy until they can be fulfilled in a godly way. We live in a highly sexualized society, and it is not hard for most of us to recount times in which we have yielded in some way to the ungodly fulfillment of sexual desire. Sexual temptation has posed a vigorous challenge since the fall of man. The apostle Paul reminds the church in Corinth of two truths. On the one hand, "the sexually immoral . . . will not inherit the kingdom of God" (1 Cor. 6:9). On the other hand, the church at Corinth was filled with those who at one time were sexually immoral but had been brought into the kingdom of God through the gospel: "But you were washed, you were sanctified, you were justified in the name of the Lord Jesus Christ and by the Spirit of our God" (v. 11). We must recognize the incongruity of sexual immorality in the Christian life, while at the same time emphasizing the grace of God for those who have sinned sexually in the past. The early church father Augustine was promiscuous before he came to faith in Christ. Sadly, his promiscuity prior to conversion gave him a negative view of sex, such that he taught that intercourse was only for the purpose of procreation. The Song of Solomon does not teach this at all. Sexual intimacy between a married couple is presented as good. The Song of Solomon also models for married couples a way of expressing their desires to each other verbally.

Whole-Bible Connections

THE GREAT BANQUET. In Song of Solomon 2:4 the woman expresses her feelings of honor because her beloved has identified himself with her in a place of public celebration: "He brought me to the banqueting house, and his banner over me was love." This verse of public honor follows the private and intimate suggestions of 2:3. Marriage is a public declaration of love, commitment, and honor to a spouse as much as it is a private commitment affording a couple godly pleasure together. This public aspect of the man's honoring the woman at a banquet house (literally "house of wine") calls to mind the Lord's Supper.[1] In the Lord's Supper, the Lord Jesus Christ has set apart bread and wine as the means by which we "proclaim the Lord's death until he comes" (1 Cor. 11:26).

Only those who belong to the Lord are to partake of this meal (1 Cor. 11:27–29), a banquet he has established as unique for his bride, the church, in order to assure her of his love and commitment. Likewise, we are to acknowledge publicly our beloved Savior before the world (Mark 8:36–38). Jesus promises us that there will come a day when his kingdom will be consummated and heaven will become a banquet house of wine, in which we will all enjoy the fruit of the vine face-to-face with our beloved Savior: "I tell you I will not drink again of this fruit of the vine until that day when I drink it new with you in my Father's kingdom" (Matt. 26:29). According to the doctrine of glorification,[2] on that day our bodies will be transformed to be like his glorious body (Phil. 3:21), and we will no longer struggle with sin, sexual or otherwise.

▶ Theological Soundings

CREATION MANDATE AND PROCREATION. In Song of Solomon 1:16 the woman shares her vision for her future life with her beloved: "Behold, you are beautiful, my beloved, truly delightful. Our couch is green." Our reading of "green" suggests that it is a way to evoke an image of a fertile marriage bed; the woman envisions her intimacy with her husband bringing forth children, all as part of a stable and strong home: "the beams of our *house* are cedar, our rafters are pine" (1:17). The classic text of the creation mandate is Genesis 1:28: "And God blessed them. And God said to them, 'Be fruitful and multiply and fill the earth and subdue it, and have dominion over the fish of the sea and over the birds of the heavens and over every living thing that moves on the earth'" (Gen. 1:28). This mandate comes as a blessing to the first married couple and includes the bearing of children. Part of God's blessing on marriage is his placing of intense sexual pleasure right at the center of the fulfillment of the creation mandate to "be fruitful and multiply." God has ordained that men and women should marry and bear children as the fruit of their sexual union. To separate sexual intercourse completely from childbearing is to put asunder what God has joined together. However, sexual intimacy is also to be enjoyed apart from the conceiving of children. Indeed, there are only so many days out of a month in which a child can be conceived, and yet there is no indication in Scripture that sex is to be limited to that window of fertility.

▶ Personal Implications

Take time to reflect on the implications of Song of Solomon 1:12–2:7 for your own life today. Consider what you have learned that might lead you to praise God, repent of sin, and trust in his gracious promises. Write down your reflections under the three headings we have considered and on the passage as a whole.

1. Gospel Glimpses

2. Whole-Bible Connections

3. Theological Soundings

4. Song of Solomon 1:12–2:7

> ### As You Finish This Unit . . .

Take a moment now to ask for the Lord's blessing and help as you continue in this study of Song of Solomon. And take a moment also to look back through this unit of study, to reflect on some key things that the Lord may be teaching you.

Definitions

[1] **Lord's Supper** – A meal of remembrance instituted by Jesus on the night of his betrayal. Christians are to observe this meal, also called Communion, in remembrance of Jesus' death. It consists of wine, symbolizing the new covenant in his blood, and bread, symbolizing his body, which was broken for his followers.

[2] **Glorification** – The work of God in believers to bring them to the ultimate and perfect stage of salvation—Christlikeness—following his justification and sanctification of them (Rom. 8:29–30). Glorification includes believers receiving imperishable resurrection bodies at Christ's return (1 Cor. 15:42–43).

Week 5: The Discipline of Waiting

Song of Solomon 2:8–17

▲

The Place of the Passage

The Song continues to progress, with the man now beckoning to the woman to come away with him. The time is not quite right, however, and the woman shows restraint. The effect of this passage is to continue to heighten the tension, as the reader awaits the consummation of this relationship in holy matrimony.

The Big Picture

The woman is sought by her beloved with cries to come away with him, but she exercises restraint for reasons of prudence, even though her desire for her beloved is strong.

Reflection and Discussion

Read through the complete passage for this study, Song of Solomon 2:8–17. Then read the passages and related questions below and record your responses.

This scene opens and closes with the voice of the woman. In the middle of the passage, she quotes the voice of her beloved. Read through the text closely and note (a) the words marking the transition between the voice of the woman and that of the man, and (b) what phrases are repeated.

Given the context of the Song as a whole and what we know about the woman's family, her life, and her insecurities, what is powerful about the image of her beloved in 2:9?

When the man calls out to the woman in 2:10–13, he makes reference to a change in season. How are these verses an apt description of marriage as a new season of life? What potential does such a description hold forth? What challenges confront the realizing of this potential?

In 2:14 the man depicts a barrier between the two lovers. What metaphor does he use to describe the distance between himself and the woman? For what does he long in this verse?

"Catch the foxes for us, the little foxes that spoil the vineyards, for our vineyards are in blossom" (v. 15). Although it is clear that the man and woman physically desire each other, there are dangers (symbolized by foxes) that must be addressed before they can come together, lest their relationship ("our vineyard") be corrupted. It is difficult to understand exactly what these "foxes" may be. What can you conceive of as "foxes" that might threaten the relationship if the man were to cross the wall (see v. 9)?

Even though at this time the woman does not respond physically to her beloved, she pledges herself to him in no uncertain terms (v. 16). What does she declare about herself and her beloved?

Read through the following three sections on *Gospel Glimpses*, *Whole-Bible Connections*, and *Theological Soundings*. Then take time to consider the *Personal Implications* these sections may have for you.

Gospel Glimpses

THE GOSPEL AND SELF-CONTROL. The gospel is the power of God for salvation (Rom. 1:16–17). Those who trust Christ for salvation are united to him spiritually and, by God's grace, are set free from the *guilt* and the *power* of sin. The apostle Paul declares, "The grace of God has appeared, bringing salvation for all people, training us to renounce ungodliness and worldly passions, and to live self-controlled, upright, and godly lives in the present age" (Titus 2:11–12; compare Gal. 5:22–23). We may not know exactly what risks or dangers are represented by the foxes in 2:15, but we do see the woman, full of passion for her beloved, nevertheless waiting until the proper time. When it comes to sexual intimacy, we must be careful to maintain two truths: Sexual intimacy is a good gift to be enjoyed in the right context and at the right time. And yet sexual urges must often be resisted by self-control so that we may live a godly life. The gospel sets us free from the power of sin so that we can exercise such self-control when necessary.

Whole Bible Connections

AN APPEAL FOR PROTECTION. The devotion of the woman to her beloved is clear from verse 16, as she declares, "My beloved is mine and I am his." But the time is not right for them to consummate their relationship, which is symbolized by a vineyard. We may not know what foxes are endangering their vineyard, but the woman calls upon her beloved to catch them. When Adam and Eve were in the garden, the Serpent appeared in order to cause harm to their relationship with God and with each other. One prominent feature of that account in Genesis 3 is that Adam is completely silent. There was a fox in his vineyard, yet he did nothing to catch it or stop it. Our heroine in the Song of Solomon longs for a better response from her beloved, and we can presume that he does not disappoint her. Men and women must look for spouses who honor God's Word and can provide spiritual encouragement.

Theological Soundings

A GODLY PURSUIT. The woman's beloved makes known to her his desire for her to join him quickly. While her voice has been primary to this point in the Song, the reader is assured that this strong young man is indeed in vigorous pursuit of the woman. A man's godly pursuit of a woman is an important aspect of displaying the capacity to love and protect her as a spouse, should they marry.

> **Personal Implications**

Take time to reflect on the implications of Song of Solomon 2:8–17 for your own life today. Consider what you have learned that might lead you to praise God, repent of sin, and trust in his gracious promises. Write down your reflections under the three headings we have considered and on the passage as a whole.

1. Gospel Glimpses

2. Whole-Bible Connections

3. Theological Soundings

4. Song of Solomon 2:8–17

As You Finish This Unit . . .

Take a moment now to ask for the Lord's blessing and help as you continue in this study of Song of Solomon. And take a moment also to look back through this unit of study, to reflect on some key things that the Lord may be teaching you.

WEEK 6: A NIGHT OF INSECURITY

Song of Solomon 3:1–5

▲

There are two dreams in the Song. The first is found in this week's passage, which comes immediately before the wedding and consummation sequence. We can tell this passage is a dream by its content and its first line, "On my bed by night, I sought him . . . but found him not" (3:1). The next dream begins at 5:2, immediately following the consummation of the wedding: "I slept, but my heart was awake," begins the woman. The content of these dreams is appropriate to the type of insecurities a bride may feel just prior to and after her wedding. The dreams share a common theme of the woman wandering in the city in search of her beloved. Watchmen of the city also appear in both dreams.

The Big Picture

The woman dreams that she must go about the city to find her beloved.

> ## Reflection and Discussion

Read through the complete passage for this study, Song of Solomon 3:1–5. Then read the passages and related questions below and record your responses.

These five verses are remarkably rich with detail, encompassing a number of scenes and encounters. Read through the verses carefully, noting the different locations of the woman and the people she encounters along the way.

In verses 1–2, how is repetition used to heighten tension? How is this tension resolved as the passage unfolds?

How is the depiction of the woman in these verses different from the way she is presented in the previous passage (2:8–17)?

In 3:4, the woman finally finds her beloved. What does she do to him? Where does she take him? Is the woman dreaming of consummating her marriage with her beloved, or of keeping him safe until the wedding day (see 1:4; 8:2)?

Why is the counsel of 3:5 appropriate at this point in the Song of Solomon?

How might one avoid "awakening love until it pleases" in our own modern context?

Read through the following three sections on *Gospel Glimpses, Whole-Bible Connections*, and *Theological Soundings*. Then take time to consider the *Personal Implications* these sections may have for you.

Gospel Glimpses

ALL THINGS FOR GOOD. The woman's dream reveals the risks involved in romantic relationships. Once a person has captured another's affections, the possibility of losing or not being able to find him or her can lead to anxiety. There are also those times in which those who have captured our affections fail us in some way or other. Worse yet, commitments are sometimes broken, resulting in great pain. In a fallen world, relationships will be fraught with these types of risks. Following Christ closely can help minimize the heartache in many cases. However, there is no guarantee that those to whom we give our heart will not cause pain and suffering. It is important to remember that those who know Christ are promised that God ultimately works all things for their good and for his glory, as the apostle Paul writes in Romans 8:28–29. *All things* includes the painful elements of life, the mistakes we make, and the wounds we incur from or give to others. God's plan to work all things for good does not mean that all things are good in and of themselves. Sin is not good. Pain is not good. Most loss is not good. But in Christ, God the Father cares for his children in the midst of trials. He uses difficulty to draw us closer to Christ, conform us more to the character of Christ, and cause us to think more of Christ than of anyone or anything else in this life.

Whole-Bible Connections

THE GOOD SHEPHERD. Human relationships are fraught with insecurity. In this passage, we see how the woman fears the loss of her beloved. Unlike regular human beings, our Savior, Jesus, assures us that we need never fear losing him: "I am the good shepherd. The good shepherd lays down his life for the sheep. He who is a hired hand and not a shepherd, who does not own the sheep, sees the wolf coming and leaves the sheep and flees, and the wolf snatches them and scatters them" (John 10:11–12). Jesus has proven his love for the flock by sacrificing his own life on our behalf, and we need not worry about his deserting us as a fickle human shepherd would. Moreover, Jesus promises to protect us against those who would try to take us from him: "I give them eternal life, and they will never perish, and no one will snatch them out of my hand" (John 10:28). Our deep longing for lasting security is ultimately fulfilled only in Jesus Christ.

Theological Soundings

PROVIDENCE. Dreams occur frequently in the Bible. Many times in Scripture, dreams are a vehicle for divine revelation. At our point in the history of redemption, we do not rely on dreams for divine revelation. We have the fullness of the Lord's revealed will for us in the Word of God. The doctrine of God's providence teaches us that God is sovereign[1] over all things for the good of his creatures. Dreams are best placed in the category of God's providence.[2] Romantic relationships impact us deeply and often produce dreams. Dreams are elusive, and we cannot place too much weight on them. However, we should be self-aware as to what is on our hearts and minds, being sure to take our concerns to God.

Persistent themes in dreams may reveal insecurities that ought to be explored under the light of God's Word.

Personal Implications

Take time to reflect on the implications of Song of Solomon 3:1–5 for your own life today. Consider what you have learned that might lead you to praise God, repent of sin, and trust in his gracious promises. Write down your reflections under the three headings we have considered and on the passage as a whole.

1. Gospel Glimpses

2. Whole-Bible Connections

3. Theological Soundings

4. Song of Solomon 3:1–5

As You Finish This Unit . . .

Take a moment now to ask for the Lord's blessing and help as you continue in this study of Song of Solomon. And take a moment also to look back through this unit of study, to reflect on some key things that the Lord may be teaching you.

Definitions

[1] **Sovereignty** – Supreme and independent power and authority. Sovereignty over all things is a distinctive attribute of God (1 Tim. 6:15–16). He directs all things to carry out his purposes (Rom. 8:28–29).

[2] **Providence** – God's good, wise, and sovereign guidance and control of all things, by which he supplies all our needs and accomplishes his holy will.

WEEK 7: THE WEDDING

Song of Solomon 3:6–5:1

The Place of the Passage

The day of the wedding has finally arrived! This wedding scene is at the center of the Song and forms an important point of transition. The themes until this point have been themes of anticipation. The themes after the wedding will be themes of renewal.

The Big Picture

The woman and her beloved consummate their relationship.

Reflection and Discussion

Read through the complete passage for this study, Song of Solomon 3:6–5:1. Then read the passages and related questions below and record your responses.

The word "What" in 3:6 is literally "Who" in Hebrew, and it is in the feminine gender. Taking this into account, it is best to read 3:6 as the man speaking about the woman coming up from the wilderness. The wilderness is a place of barrenness and of hostile forces of nature. Yet the woman emerges refined, perfumed, and ready to be a blessing to her future spouse. The woman is seen as a garden of rest and refreshment for the man amid a hostile world.[1] Man and woman were created for a perfect world in the garden of Eden, and there is a sense in which the blessings of God upon marriage are a foretaste of the restoration of that perfect home. In 4:12–5:1, both the man and the woman employ a garden metaphor. Compare and contrast how the two of them use this metaphor to describe their wedding and the consummation of their love.

Verse 7 contains a sharp shift marked by "Behold!" as the scene shifts to a procession of Solomon, carried on a couch ("litter"; 3:7) on the day of *his* wedding (vv. 7–11). This is the only time Solomon has an active role in the Song. In our reading of the Song of Solomon, supported especially by the Hebrew text of 3:6 (with "Who" referring to the shepherdess; see discussion above), Solomon is not appearing here because he is the groom featured in this book. Rather, Solomon appears here as a literary foil, providing a point of contrast. What our couple enjoys is more glorious than the wealth and power of Solomon's kingdom. The epilogue at the end of the Song contains an allusion to the day of the wedding, with the woman again "coming up from the wilderness" (8:5), this time with her beloved on her arm. Then, in 8:11–12 the woman compares her relationship with her beloved to the relationships Solomon had with his wives and concubines. Hers is superior to the royal king's because it is exclusive.

The implications of these comparisons are clear. First, the woman's beauty is more glorious than Solomon clothed in all his splendor. Second, the wedding of a shepherd and a shepherdess, though they are ordinary people, surpasses the glory of King Solomon. His wedding procession is marked by signs of power and money. The two lovers of the Song, by contrast, have a wedding marked by their own pure love and delight in each other. This pure love is to be desired more than power or money. Read the description of Solomon (3:7–11). Write down the words, phrases, and descriptions associated with his power and wealth.

In 4:1–16 the voice of the man breaks forth powerfully. These 16 verses comprise the longest section in which the man speaks in the Song. They include his praise for his bride's beauty (vv. 1–7), a request for her to go away with him (v. 8), a description of how she has captured his heart (v. 9), another section praising her beauty and comparing her to a locked garden (vv. 10–15), and final pleas for the forces of nature to come and unleash the treasures of the locked garden (v. 16). Read verses 1–7 and 10–11. Of the many metaphors used to describe the woman, which do you find most compelling to modern readers? Which are most distant?

There is progression in the Song. In 2:8–17, what physical barrier stands between the woman and her beloved? By contrast, what barrier separates them in 4:1–3? What does the change in these physical barriers indicate?

The beloved has described seven aspects of the woman's body, a number of perfection. With this complete examination of her beauty he exclaims, "You are altogether beautiful, my love; there is no flaw in you" (4:7). Presented as an ideal for married couples, what do these verses suggest for husbands and wives in times of intimacy?

In 4:12 we find a series of evocative metaphors the man uses to describe his bride. If there is any doubt as to what is referenced in these metaphors, the woman seems to remove it in 4:16b: "Let my beloved come to his garden, and eat its choicest fruits." In our age of sexual coarseness, we should not miss the beautiful way in which the Scriptures speak of the consummation of this marriage. The images are powerful and clear, perhaps even so much so as to embarrass some readers. Nevertheless, they are tasteful and appropriately restrained. What four verbs does the man employ in 5:1 to describe the consummation he experiences with his bride?

How do we see this consummation of marriage affirmed as a good and godly thing at the close of 5:1?

Read through the following three sections on *Gospel Glimpses, Whole-Bible Connections*, and *Theological Soundings*. Then take time to consider the *Personal Implications* these sections may have for you.

▶ Gospel Glimpses

PERFECT IN GOD'S SIGHT. In 4:7 the man is filled with passion and declares that his bride is perfect: "There is no flaw in you." Filled with passion for his bride, the man sees her as absolutely perfect. The ideal for marriage is for this type of complete acceptance to characterize every aspect of the relationship. Times of sexual intimacy bolster the marriage bond, making it easier to look past what in reality may be imperfections of one kind or another. The man's complete affirmation of his wife is a picture of a much more radical and permanent affirmation that believers receive from the Lord. Our Savior went to the cross to identify with our sinful imperfections so that we might become completely righteous in him. Theologians call this the "great exchange," the act of Christ's taking our place on the cross so that we may be considered completely righteous in the sight of God: "For our sake he made him to be sin who knew no sin, so that in him we might become the righteousness of God" (2 Cor. 5:21).

46

> ## Whole-Bible Connections

KING SOLOMON, MARRIAGE, AND CHRIST. God provides foundational instruction for all of the kings of Israel in Deuteronomy 17. In 17:17 the Lord warns that Israel's king "shall not acquire many wives for himself, lest his heart turn away, nor shall he acquire for himself excessive silver and gold." No king of Israel violated these commands more than Solomon. First Kings 11:3 records that Solomon "had 700 wives, who were princesses, and 300 concubines." And every year Solomon received in tribute the equivalent of 25 tons of gold (1 Kings 10:14). One of the most important lessons to take away from the Song of Solomon is that God offers extraordinary blessing to ordinary men and women who commit themselves to godly marriage. The pleasure and glory of such a union surpasses anything Solomon ever experienced. The Song teaches us that a lifelong marriage to the same spouse is the pathway to the richest blessings. There is a spiritual, emotional, and psychological depth intended for the sexual relationship that cannot be cultivated with multiple partners. It takes an exclusive commitment to one's husband or wife to discover truly the deepest joys God intends for sexual intimacy. Anything else is a fleeting and ultimately painful substitute. This message must be promoted in an age that constantly heralds the fleeting pleasures of promiscuity and sexual experimentation. Further, the glory of a godly marriage is intended to point to the greater glory of Christ himself. Every husband will fall short of Christ. King Solomon was a moral failure as Israel's king. But, thankfully, we have One greater than Solomon (Matt. 12:42) who perfectly kept the law of God for the people of God. Christ loved the church, his bride, even unto death.

> ## Theological Soundings

SEX, MONEY, AND POWER. The Scriptures warn against the allure and abuse of sex, money, and power. Solomon's reign was characterized by all three to an extreme. Christ, by contrast, held fast in the face of temptation to exalt himself, so that he could save us from our sins (Matt. 4:1–11). In the book of Revelation, the city of Babylon is judged for her adulteries and excessive luxuries (Rev. 18:3). This ungodly city is adorned in purple, gold, and pearls (Rev. 18:16). The bride of Christ, by contrast, is clothed in "fine linen, bright and pure" (Rev. 19:8). There is a simplicity and purity commended to the people of God in this contrast, as well as a warning not to be seduced by the money, sex, or power of this world. The woman in the Song of Solomon enjoys face-to-face intimacy with her beloved in a way that Solomon could never enjoy with all of his wives, and the church similarly enjoys a face-to-face intimacy with the Lord (2 Cor. 3:18) that cannot be surpassed by all of the pleasures, riches, and power of this world.

Personal Implications

Take time to reflect on the implications of Song of Solomon 3:6–5:1 for your own life today. Consider what you have learned that might lead you to praise God, repent of sin, and trust in his gracious promises. Write down your reflections under the three headings we have considered and on the passage as a whole.

1. Gospel Glimpses

2. Whole-Bible Connections

3. Theological Soundings

4. Song of Solomon 3:6–5:1

As You Finish This Unit . . .

Take a moment now to ask for the Lord's blessing and help as you continue in this study of Song of Solomon. And take a moment also to look back through this unit of study, to reflect on some key things that the Lord may be teaching you.

Definition

[1] **World** – In Scripture, the context determines the meaning of this term. The physical world is God's creation of the earth and everything in it. "World" can refer to all of humanity (John 3:16) or to the unbelieving, godless world system (John 1:10), often as an adjective, "worldly" (1 Cor. 1:26).

Week 8: The Dream

Song of Solomon 5:2–6:3

▲

The Place of the Passage

With the wedding past and the relationship consummated, we now see insecurities and difficulties to be faced in the relationship, especially in the sexual dimension. Relationships are not mechanical; they are dynamic. There will be times when the desires of one spouse do not align with the desires of the other, which can lead to tension. This week's passage is the second dream in the Song of Solomon (compare 3:1–5). The ambiguity of a dream makes it an ideal vehicle to express the imprecision of the sexual relationship of a married couple.

The Big Picture

In this dream, the man seeks intimacy with his bride, but she delays. By the time she readies herself, he has departed, and she runs through the streets to find him.

> ## Reflection and Discussion

Read through the complete passage for this study, Song of Solomon 5:2–6:3. Then read the passages and related questions below and record your responses.

What indications are there in the text that these verses are describing a dream?

In 5:2–6 we see that this dream is about an encounter where the timing of the couple's desires for intimacy is not aligned. This is often the case in a marriage relationship, and therefore this text comes as an encouragement to married couples. Even with the great passion this couple experiences in their consummation, they still experience the ordinary ups and downs of intimacy in their married life. At what point in these verses does the woman's desire shift toward her husband?

What does she indicate was the reason for her delay in responding to her husband's entreaty for intimacy?

Verse 4 marks a sudden shift in the woman's disposition toward her husband. How is this expressed in the poetry?

Once again the Song captures much in just a few verses. In 5:6, when we suspect the tension could be relieved, the woman opens the door to her beloved, only to find him gone. This leads to another scene in the dream. How does the woman respond to her beloved's absence? What is suggested by the treatment she receives from the watchmen of the city?

What does 5:7 suggest about the types of feelings the woman experiences when contemplating losing her husband?

In 5:8 the woman calls out to the daughters of Jerusalem to deliver a message to her beloved if they find him: "tell him I am sick with love." They respond by asking her to justify why she is sick with love, asking what sets her beloved apart from other men. This leads to the most elaborate physical description that the woman offers of her beloved. The woman, like the man in 4:1–7, praises the totality of her beloved's body. Which metaphors in these verses (vv. 10–16) are most compelling to you as a modern reader?

By the time we reach 6:1–3, the tension of the dream has faded away. Compared to 5:2–8, what tone is conveyed in 6:2–3?

Read through the following three sections on *Gospel Glimpses*, *Whole-Bible Connections*, and *Theological Soundings*. Then take time to consider the *Personal Implications* these sections may have for you.

▶ Gospel Glimpses

PATIENCE. As soon as the marriage is consummated, we behold the couple, in the context of the woman's dream, acting somewhat fickle. When the man desires intimacy, the woman cannot be bothered. When she is finally captivated, she rises to find him gone. The ensuing search leads her to harm at the hands of the watchmen, only adding further frustration to the situation. The dream of the woman shows that marriage does not afford couples an uninterrupted stream of physical intimacy. Married couples live together as fallen people in a fallen world. Desires do not always align perfectly, and circumstances do not always provide opportunities for intimacy when desires are present. In Jesus Christ, the Holy Spirit works the fruit of patience in us. For married couples, this will include patience in times where one's own desires are not matched by the spouse's or by the right opportunity. It is also of note that the man does not force himself on his bride. Sexual union in marriage should be entered into with the joyful consent of both spouses.

Whole-Bible Connections

A ROBE OF RIGHTEOUSNESS. "Veil" in 5:7 is not the same as the garment mentioned in 1:7; 4:1, 3. In 5:7 the garment referred to is likely a light and flimsy undergarment. In this dream, the woman is running through the streets inappropriately dressed. In this state she is discovered by the watchmen, who then remove this cloak from her. Seen in such light, this is a rather graphic and humiliating assault on the woman that reveals the depth of insecurity present in her dream. It is truly a humiliating scene: when the woman runs out to look for her husband, she is accosted and exposed. The fear of being exposed is rooted in a deeper spiritual reality. Our first parents, Adam and Eve, wore no clothes because they knew no sin or shame. When they sinned against the Lord, however, they fled from his presence in shame and attempted to cover themselves with fig leaves. To address their shame, the Lord himself clothed them with animal skins. Significantly, the first recorded shedding of blood in Scripture is the shedding of the blood of an animal to address the shame of Adam and Eve. The Lord's ultimate plan was to shed the blood not of an animal but of his own Son to atone for our sins. As a result, we are clothed with the righteousness[1] of Christ. As Isaiah prophesied, "He has clothed me with the garments of salvation; he has covered me with the robe of righteousness" (Isa. 61:10). Our deepest needs and insecurities are ultimately resolved only through the assurance that the Lord himself has clothed us with the righteousness of Christ. We need not fear or be ashamed, if we are in Christ.

Theological Soundings

HUMAN NATURE. It is important not to be naive about human nature. Sexual intimacy impacts human beings, both male and female. In the dream, the woman is sick with love because she has been physically united with her spouse but is now separated from him. It is God's design for those who are so joined to remain together. Deviating from this design will cause pain and insecurity.

Personal Implications

Take time to reflect on the implications of Song of Solomon 5:2–6:3 for your own life today. Consider what you have learned that might lead you to praise God, repent of sin, and trust in his gracious promises. Write down your reflections under the three headings we have considered and on the passage as a whole.

1. Gospel Glimpses

2. Whole-Bible Connections

3. Theological Soundings

4. Song of Solomon 5:2–6:3

As You Finish This Unit . . .

Take a moment now to ask for the Lord's blessing and help as you continue in this study of Song of Solomon. And take a moment also to look back through this unit of study, to reflect on some key things that the Lord may be teaching you.

Definition

[1] **Righteousness** – The quality of being morally right and without sin. God imputes righteousness to (justifies) those who trust in Jesus Christ.

WEEK 9: RENEWED CONTEMPLATION

Song of Solomon 6:4–12

▲

The Place of the Passage

In the next two sections of the poem, the man and woman renew their relationship. In 6:4–12, the man once again praises the woman, but this time his praise is different. He shows a deeper appreciation of her character than we have seen to this point in the poem, demonstrating that growth in the relationship has occurred.

The Big Picture

The husband praises his wife for her strength and dignity.

Reflection and Discussion

Read through the complete passage for this study, Song of Solomon 6:4–12. Then read the passages and related questions below and record your responses.

In verse 4 the man says that his wife is as beautiful as Tirzah and Jerusalem. Tirzah was the original capital of the northern kingdom of Israel. Jerusalem was the capital of the southern kingdom of Judah. The man also says that her beauty is as "awesome as an army with banners," a phrase framing the whole speech with overtones of great strength. What do these comparisons say about how the man's understanding of his wife has developed over the course of their relationship?

The eyes of a person are a window into his or her soul. In verse 5, how does the man say he feels when he looks intently into the eyes of his wife? How does this show progression from his looking into her eyes in 4:9?

In verses 5–7 the man returns to praising his wife's physical appearance, this time focusing only on her face. How does he describe his wife's face?

In verses 8 and 9 the man says he prefers his spouse to 60 queens and 80 concubines. This is likely an allusion to Solomon's many wives and concubines, with the point being that the man would prefer an exclusive relationship with his bride to multiple relationships with other women. He has chosen this woman above all others. How does verse 9 expand upon the man's appreciation of her character? To what does he compare her, and what virtues does he extol in her?

In this passage the man's voice has been dominant. However, the woman's voice returns in verses 11–12. She was taking a walk in nature (v. 11) before suddenly being surprised to encounter her husband (v. 12). How does she describe him in verse 12? What does this description say about the depth of appreciation she has for his character?

Read through the following three sections on *Gospel Glimpses*, *Whole-Bible Connections*, and *Theological Soundings*. Then take time to consider the *Personal Implications* these sections may have for you.

Gospel Glimpses

GROWTH IN GRACE. The Bible instructs husbands to "live with your wives in an understanding way, showing honor to the woman as the weaker vessel, since they are heirs with you of the grace of life, so that your prayers may not be hindered" (1 Pet. 3:7–8). Dwelling with understanding is a broad concept. It certainly includes being mindful that women are typically not as physically strong as men, as Peter notes. But it means more than this. To live in an understanding way likely includes growth in a man's understanding of his wife's personality, gifts, strengths, and temperament. In the Song of Solomon, the man shows that he has grown in his understanding of his bride. He uses images to describe her strength and dignity, in addition to her physical beauty. As the poem unfolds, we will see that this deeper understanding of his wife only strengthens their capacity for sexual intimacy.

FREEDOM FROM SHAME. In the garden of Eden, Adam and Eve were originally created naked and unashamed. When they sinned, they covered themselves with fig leaves to hide their shame. Now their relationship would be strained, and this danger would persist for all men and women who would come after them. In the Song of Solomon, we can see from the woman's words to her husband that reconciliation is possible. She freely expresses her desire for him without shame. This type of reconciliation to a spouse comes most naturally when one is first reconciled to God and therefore free of shame and guilt. The Lord offers married couples a new and restored pathway not only to be sexually intimate with each other but also to express those desires verbally without shame.

Whole-Bible Connections

CHARM IS DECEPTIVE AND BEAUTY IS FLEETING. This passage provides an essential balancing perspective for the Song of Solomon. The Song gives full place to sexual desire and intimacy, but these verses show that sexual intimacy is not separate from a deep admiration of character. A godly husband will find that the character of his wife accentuates her attractiveness. The respect and reverence the man has for his wife in these verses call to mind the respect a husband gives his godly wife in Proverbs 31:29: "Many women have done excellently, but you surpass them all" (see vv. 10–31). As the writer of Proverbs says, "Charm is deceitful and beauty is vain, but a woman who fears the LORD is to be praised" (31:30). Peter instructs wives not to be content with outward beauty but to focus on the development of godly character: "Let your adorning be the hidden . . . beauty of a gentle and quiet spirit, which in God's sight is very precious" (1 Pet. 3:4). The development of godly character is essential in a relationship. Let us not put asunder what God has joined together when it comes to the complementary roles that romance and godly character play in a marriage.

Theological Soundings

THE EXCLUSIVITY OF MARRIAGE. This week's passage emphasizes a depth of relationship between a man and a woman possible only in marriage between one man and one woman forever. In Genesis 2:24–25 we read, "A man shall leave his father and his mother and hold fast to his wife, and they shall become one flesh. And the man and his wife were both naked and were not ashamed." Becoming one flesh in marriage speaks not only to physical intimacy but to emotional and psychological intimacy as well. This type of deep knowledge takes time to develop. It also takes a willingness to grow, to persevere, to be patient, and to forgive. Those who give themselves to this vision of marriage will find that they have a relationship longed for by those who appear to have it all in the eyes of the world but who have never really known true love between a man and a woman, as God designed it (Song 6:9). Before entering into marriage, we must ensure that our future spouse shares the same vision for marriage that we do. Parents also need to understand that God is forming a new family through such marriages, with a distinct head of household in the man, and a wife whose priority is her husband.

Personal Implications

Take time to reflect on the implications of Song of Solomon 6:4–12 for your own life today. Consider what you have learned that might lead you to praise God, repent of sin, and trust in his gracious promises. Write down your reflections under the three headings we have considered and on the passage as a whole.

1. Gospel Glimpses

2. Whole-Bible Connections

3. Theological Soundings

4. Song of Solomon 6:4–12

> ### As You Finish This Unit . . .

Take a moment now to ask for the Lord's blessing and help as you continue in this study of Song of Solomon. And take a moment also to look back through this unit of study, to reflect on some key things that the Lord may be teaching you.

Week 10: Renewed Consummation

Song of Solomon 6:13–8:4

The Place of the Passage

Following a season of contemplation, the couple once more enter into sexual expression of their love for each other. The language of this section is even more romantically exuberant than the description of the couple's wedding night. The literary center of the Song is the consummation of the marriage. The romantic climax of the Song occurs toward the end of the poem, just before the epilogue. This is instructive, for it is after the couple has experienced the insecurities, trials, and forgiveness of marriage that they are able to enter even more deeply into the romantic pleasures of marriage. Today's culture suggests repeatedly that romance is something that flourishes among couples with few obligations in general and no lasting obligations to each other. The Song of Solomon, however, would have us know that romance is best cultivated over a lifetime of commitment. Within God's design, a husband and wife can be assured that the romance of their relationship can be rekindled.

The Big Picture

Having come to a deeper appreciation of their character and commitment, the man and the woman enjoy deeper romantic intimacy.

> ### Reflection and Discussion

Read through the complete passage for this study, Song of Solomon 6:13–8:4. Then read the passages and related questions below and record your responses.

Read 7:1–3. The husband describes his wife by beginning at the feet and work-ing his way up. The only articles of clothing mentioned are sandals, which suggests that all her other clothing has been set aside. The Hebrew word for "thighs" likely refers to the buttocks, while the "navel" is likely a euphemism for the entire genital area. The husband compares the enjoyment of sexual intimacy with his wife to the drinking of fine wine (7:2), a metaphor the wife also uses to encourage his indulgence of her (7:9; 8:2). This is the most explicit language of the entire poem, and it is given by divine revelation. We see that God desires to foster this type of relational intimacy among married couples. Creative, verbal expressions of sexual delight are appropriate for married couples. Yet this type of expression is to be reserved for the context of marriage. The Lord has given us the Song of Solomon so that those who remain chaste need not wonder about the power of romantic love. All that we need to know about such love is given to us in this Song in sufficient detail.

How do the metaphors of 7:4 and 7:5 exalt the woman's dignity?

What is the significance of the palm tree metaphor in 7:7?

How does the language of 7:1–9 stand apart from the crass sexual language of our modern culture?

Why is the relational security of the marriage commitment the only safe place for such expressions of intimacy and affection?

In 7:10 the woman speaks of her husband's desire for her. This word for "desire" occurs only here and in Genesis 3:16 and 4:7. Compare the context of the word in Genesis 3:16; 4:7 to its use in Song of Solomon 7:10.

Read 8:1–4. What does the woman mean when she exclaims, "Oh that you were like a brother to me who nursed at my mother's breasts"?

How does 8:2 suggest that this romantic relationship is right, good, and pure?

What does 8:1–4 suggest about the role of family and friends in choosing a spouse (compare 3:4)?

Read through the following three sections on *Gospel Glimpses*, *Whole-Bible Connections*, and *Theological Soundings*. Then take time to consider the *Personal Implications* these sections may have for you.

Gospel Glimpses

AS GOD IN CHRIST FORGAVE YOU. We see in these verses the capacity for exuberance and celebration in marriage, even after a season of trial, difficulty, or insecurity. The gospel provides a continual basis for us to "[bear] with one another in love" (Eph. 4:2) and to forgive one another as God in Christ has forgiven us (Eph. 4:32). Marriage will not offer an uninterrupted stream of sexual passion with the attendant verbal affirmations. Instead, couples will go through seasons of disagreement and difficulty, which, when lived out under the power of the gospel, will afford a basis for reconciliation that will strengthen their relationship. This gospel dynamic in marriage is a key to fueling the type of passion we see in this passage. Couples who marry on the basis of sexual attraction alone, lacking a common spiritual foundation, will, over time, find their passion declining because the grace of God is not renewing their love for each other regularly. This is why it is vital for believers to marry "in the Lord" (1 Cor. 7:39).

Whole-Bible Connections

THE REVERSAL OF THE CURSE. In 7:10 the woman exclaims, "I am my beloved's, and his desire is for me." This rare biblical word for *desire* also occurs in Genesis 3:16: "To the woman he said, 'I will surely multiply your pain in childbearing; in pain you shall bring forth children. Your desire shall be contrary to your husband, but he shall rule over you'" (see also Gen. 4:7). God spoke these words to Eve as a curse for her disobedience to the Lord's command not to eat from the tree of the knowledge of good and evil (Gen. 2:17; 3:6). The sin of Adam and Eve led not only to alienation from God but also to relational strife. By the use of the same word for *desire* in Song of Solomon 7:10 and Genesis 3:6, we can see the abundance of God's grace for marriage. While perfection in this life is not possible, and couples will always wrestle with selfishness, in Jesus Christ the Lord offers a pathway for peace and intimacy in marriage. Remarkably, the gospel affords every marriage the potential to recapture what was lost in Eden and a foretaste of what awaits every believer in the new heavens and the new earth. Although Adam and Eve and their progeny were cursed in the garden, "Christ redeemed us from the curse of the law by becoming a curse for us—for it is written, 'Cursed is everyone who is hanged on a tree'" (Gal. 3:13). Those who trust in Jesus Christ receive the promised blessing of the Holy Spirit. It is through continual dependence upon the Holy Spirit in marriage (and in other relationships as well) that we realize the fruit that God intends for our good and his glory.

Theological Soundings

THE BODY AS A TEMPLE OF THE HOLY SPIRIT. When the apostle Paul exhorts the Corinthians to flee from sexual immorality, he reminds them that their bodies are temples[1] of the Holy Spirit: "Flee from sexual immorality. Every other sin a person commits is outside the body, but the sexually immoral person sins against his own body. Or do you not know that your body is a temple of the Holy Spirit within you, whom you have from God? You are not your own, for you were bought with a price. So glorify God in your body" (1 Cor. 6:18–20). If we are believers in Christ, our bodies are to be reserved for holy use because God himself dwells within us. The Lord has made sex in marriage holy, and it is to be enjoyed with his blessing and under his instruction. When contemplating marriage, couples must honestly ask themselves whether their partner is a temple of the Holy Spirit. Are they genuine believers in the Lord Jesus Christ? If not, then they must heed Paul's warning to the Corinthians not to be "unequally yoked with unbelievers" (2 Cor. 6:14). The basis for Paul's instruction is that the believer and the unbeliever participate in two different spiritual worlds, one light and the other dark, that are in conflict with each other. "For what partnership has righteousness with lawlessness? Or what fellowship has light with darkness? What accord has Christ with Belial? Or what portion does a believer share with an unbeliever? What agreement has the temple of God with idols? For we are the temple of the living God" (2 Cor. 6:14–16).

Personal Implications

Take time to reflect on the implications of Song of Solomon 6:13–8:4 for your own life today. Consider what you have learned that might lead you to praise God, repent of sin, and trust in his gracious promises. Write down your reflections under the three headings we have considered and on the passage as a whole.

1. Gospel Glimpses

2. Whole-Bible Connections

3. Theological Soundings

4. Song of Solomon 6:13–8:4

> ### As You Finish This Unit . . .

Take a moment now to ask for the Lord's blessing and help as you continue in this study of Song of Solomon. And take a moment also to look back through this unit of study, to reflect on some key things that the Lord may be teaching you.

Definition

[1] **Temple** – A place set aside as holy because of God's presence there. Solomon built the first temple of the Lord in Jerusalem, to replace the portable tabernacle. This temple was later destroyed by the Babylonians, rebuilt, and destroyed again by the Romans.

Week 11: Epilogue

Song of Solomon 8:5–14

▲

The Place of the Passage

This week's passage is the epilogue to the Song of Solomon, which brings the book to a fitting conclusion by summarizing its major themes. It forms an inclusio[1] with the prologue section (Song 1:2–2:7). Only in the prologue and the epilogue do the woman's brothers (1:6; 8:8–9) appear. The same word is used for "companions" in 1:7 and 8:13, also occurring only in the prologue and epilogue. Further, it is only in these sections that we find the phrase "my own vineyard," in both cases used powerfully as the woman compares herself to others (1:6; 8:11–12). Here the great themes of the book are revisited from a more complete vantage point. The reader for the first time encounters the only direct reference to the Lord in the Song of Solomon: the reader now learns that the power of human love is a marker of an even greater love, the love of God himself—love is the "very flame of the Lord" (8:6). The poem ends with a final delightful entreaty from the woman to her lover that he "make haste" to be with her (8:14), suggesting that the romance continues long after the poem comes to a close.

The Big Picture

The woman reflects on the superiority of her love for her beloved.

Reflection and Discussion

Read through the complete passage for this study, Song of Solomon 8:5–14. Then read the passages and related questions below and record your responses.

Read 8:5. What motifs from the Song of Solomon as a whole are represented in this one verse?

Read 8:6–7. In these verses the woman longs for her husband to always be mindful of her love by setting her as a seal on his heart. A seal in the ancient world conveyed ownership. She wants all to know that this man is *her* man; he enjoys her love and belongs to her alone. What metaphors does the woman use to describe love?

How do the metaphors used here to describe love differ from popular conceptions of love today? What can we learn from these ancient metaphors?

Read 8:8–9. The Song of Solomon is a part of the Bible's wisdom literature, which cultivates skill for living as God commands. In these verses, voices pose a question to the woman; the implication is that this is a poem of advice—all along the woman and the man have been sharing their experience of love to advise us, to offer us wisdom. These voices have a little sister who has not reached sexual maturity (she has no breasts). They pose the rhetorical question, "What shall we do for our sister on the day when she is spoken for?" The meaning of their answer is not absolutely certain, but it is widely held that the metaphor of a wall refers to chastity, while the door refers to being unchaste. If this is true, what does verse 9 suggest that they will do for the sister if she is inclined toward great chastity and reservation (a wall) in her relationships with the opposite sex?

What does it suggest they will do if she is inclined toward great openness or unchaste behavior with the opposite sex?

In verse 10 the woman says that *she too* was a wall (i.e., once inclined toward chastity and reservation). How is this self-description in keeping with 2:8–17?

In verses 11–12 the woman speaks of her body and her relationship with her husband as a vineyard. She compares herself to Solomon, who had great wealth and many women but could not find true intimacy because he strayed from God's design. What are the implications of her comparison? As part of the epilogue, what does this comparison suggest with regard to what we should value most in a marriage relationship?

_____

_____

_____

_____

_____

_____

In verses 13–14 the Song of Solomon concludes with a final brief exchange between the woman and her husband. What do these verses suggest about their future?

_____

_____

_____

_____

_____

What do they suggest about the nature of lifelong marital relationships?

_____

_____

_____

_____

_____

Read through the following three sections on *Gospel Glimpses*, *Whole-Bible Connections*, and *Theological Soundings*. Then take time to consider the *Personal Implications* these sections may have for you.

Gospel Glimpses

ENDURING LOVE. True love endures, yet it is the nature of human beings to falter in their love. The gospel, however, enables us to love as we ought to love. First, because of the gospel we can find forgiveness for our lack of love. A failure to love is always first a sin against the God who commands that we love our neighbors as ourselves. When we fail to love as we ought, we are called to repent and believe the gospel once again, so that we might draw upon the Holy Spirit to enable us to love from the place of freedom in Christ rather than from the place of guilt and obligation. Second, we also find in the gospel the greatest example of love that the world has ever seen. The Lord Jesus Christ "loved [us] and gave himself for [us]" (Gal. 2:20). He loved us unto death, and he calls us to persevere in love for others.

Whole-Bible Connections

COVENANT FAITHFULNESS. The woman longs to be set as a seal upon the heart and the arm of the man (Song 8:6). A seal in the ancient world signified ownership. Because of her great love for the man, she wants him to remember that he belongs to her, and she also wants others to know that he belongs to her. The love sealed in a human marriage covenant[2] is intended by God to point us toward his own covenant love for his people. Like the love of the woman for her beloved, God's covenant love for his people is as "strong as death," jealous, and unquenchable. In the Old Testament we see this illustrated when God enacts a ceremony with Abraham to confirm his covenant promises to him (Gen. 15:1–21). God asks Abraham to sacrifice animals and make a pathway between them. Normally, both parties of the covenant would walk through those animals as a way of signifying that if the covenant were broken, the price would be death—the curse for breaking the covenant. But in God's covenant with Abraham, there is a major difference: God himself symbolically walks through the animals. Abraham does not walk through them at all. God will be the one who will keep this covenant completely. Even though Abraham and his spiritual descendants would sin, they would not violate this covenant in a way that would lead to their ultimate separation from God, nor would they bear the ultimate consequence. As the biblical story unfolds, it becomes clear that it will be the Son of God who bears the curse of the covenant in place of the people of God: "Christ redeemed us from the curse of the law by becoming a curse for us—for it is written, 'Cursed is everyone who is hanged on a tree'—so that in Christ Jesus the blessing of Abraham might come to the Gentiles, so that we might receive the promised Spirit through faith" (Gal. 3:13–14).

LOVE IS THE FLAME OF THE LORD. In Song of Solomon 8:6 the flashes of love are said to be the "flashes of fire, the very flame of the Lord." This is the only explicit reference to the Lord in the Song. Fittingly, at the end of the poem, we are told that when we behold the idea of human love in marriage, we are actually looking at a signpost pointing us to the love of God himself. The apostle Paul advances this teaching further when he says that the mysterious union between a man and a woman in marriage is intended to point to Christ's union with his church: "This mystery is profound, and I am saying that it refers to Christ and the church" (Eph. 5:32). The apostle John writes that it is the incarnation and crucifixion of Christ that exemplifies the inextinguishable love of God for his people: "In this the love of God was made manifest among us, that God sent his only Son into the world, so that we might live through him. In this is love, not that we have loved God but that he loved us and sent his Son to be the propitiation for our sins" (1 John 4:9–10).

Theological Soundings

DOCTRINE OF SCRIPTURE. The Song of Solomon is part of the canon[3] of Scripture. The apostle Paul writes that "All Scripture is breathed out by God and profitable for teaching, for reproof, for correction, and for training in righteousness, that the man of God may be complete, equipped for every good work" (2 Tim. 3:16–17). All of the language of the Song—its vivid images, metaphors, romantic interchanges, and sage advice—were "breathed out" by the Holy Spirit. Human language is a divine gift from God, and he employs the full riches of human language to communicate his wisdom to us. When we interpret Scripture, we must take into account the type of language being used in order to interpret it correctly. Paul would also have us see that the Song of Solomon was given so that we might be "complete, equipped for every good work." On the one hand, the Song of Solomon has at times made people uncomfortable because of its directness. Yet this direct teaching, correction, and training is needed if this book is to have its full effect. On the other hand, the Song of Solomon has sometimes been handled irreverently and crassly. It is divinely inspired, holy literature, and the teaching about sexuality in the Song is to be treated as holy and used properly for the building up of God's people.

Personal Implications

Take time to reflect on the implications of Song of Solomon 8:5–14 for your own life today. Consider what you have learned that might lead you to praise God, repent of sin, and trust in his gracious promises. Write down your reflections under the three headings we have considered and on the passage as a whole.

1. Gospel Glimpses

2. Whole-Bible Connections

3. Theological Soundings

4. Song of Solomon 8:5–14

> ### As You Finish This Unit . . .

Take a moment now to ask for the Lord's blessing and help as you continue in this study of Song of Solomon. And take a moment also to look back through this unit of study, to reflect on some key things that the Lord may be teaching you.

Definitions

[1] **Inclusio** – A pair of literary "bookends" that begin and end a text with similar material.

[2] **Covenant** – A binding agreement between two parties, typically involving a formal statement of their relationship, a list of stipulations and obligations for both parties, a list of witnesses to the agreement, and a list of curses for unfaithfulness and blessings for faithfulness to the agreement. The OT is more properly understood as the old covenant, meaning the agreement established between God and his people prior to the coming of Jesus Christ and the establishment of the new covenant (NT).

[3] **Canon** – The list of writings recognized as Scripture, that is, regarded as inspired by God and authoritative in all areas of doctrine and practice. Criteria for canonical books include: (1) apostolic authority (was the book written by or associated with an apostle?); (2) universal acceptance by the church; and (3) unity of message (is the message of the book consistent with other books recognized as inspired?).

WEEK 12: SUMMARY AND CONCLUSION

▲

The Song of Solomon is a divinely inspired book of wisdom that speaks directly to love in marriage. The Song calls readers to embrace the goodness of sexual intimacy in marriage while at the same time warning against arousing sexual desires outside of or before marriage. The Song of Solomon is a clear corrective to the worldly notion that sexual pleasure is best enjoyed with many partners. We see in the Song an increase in sexual intimacy and intensity as the marriage relationship matures in ways possible only in an exclusive lifelong commitment. The Song offers great encouragement to couples who, though ordinary in the eyes of the world, can be assured that, with God's blessing in Christ, they too can enjoy a love so great that "many waters cannot quench" it (8:7).

The Song provides a paradigm for love in marriage that recognizes the key role of the cultivation and appreciation of godly character and verbal expression in order to support sexual intimacy. The book also provides a helpful realism toward marriage by presenting the insecurities and trials present in any marriage. Within the canon of Holy Scripture, the Song of Solomon is especially noteworthy for offering a female perspective on sexuality. This perspective is an encouragement to women and a source of great insight to men who seek to be godly and loving husbands. Globally, some cultures and religions diminish the legitimacy of sexual desire among women; the Song of Solomon teaches otherwise.

The unmarried Christian is helped by the Song of Solomon because it provides divine insight into areas of life that otherwise cannot be accessed righteously. While the Song of Solomon may stoke the desire for romantic love, it can also serve as ample warning not to "awaken" love before it is the proper time to do so. The presentation of the power of love may serve as an avenue to explore how old wounds incurred in relationships may require further gospel healing. Lastly, by reading and understanding the Song of Solomon, the single Christian can be equipped to support God's institution of marriage as a member of God's family. As the apostle Paul aptly demonstrates, one need not be married to have great insight and wisdom on marriage.

The Song of Solomon ultimately points toward Jesus Christ as the church's Bridegroom. Love is the "very flame of the LORD" (8:6). Marriage as an institution is temporary—as powerful as this love is on earth, it will not be experienced in the same way in the new heavens and the new earth. When the heavenly Bridegroom has fully consummated his loving ministry to his bride, the church, there will be no need for the witness of marriage to point to Christ's love for the church. In that day, faith in the Bridegroom will have turned to sight, and the foretaste of glory in marriage will have found its fulfillment in the heavenly banquet.

▶ Gospel Glimpses

How has the Holy Spirit used your study of the Song of Solomon to enrich your understanding of the gospel?

How has your study of the Song of Solomon deepened your appreciation of the need for couples to marry in the Lord and share a common faith in Jesus Christ?

In what aspects of your own character do you wish to grow through your study of the Song of Solomon?

Whole-Bible Connections

The apostle Paul writes in Ephesians 5:31–32, "'A man shall leave his father and mother and hold fast to his wife, and the two shall become one flesh.' This mystery is profound, and I am saying that it refers to Christ and the church." How has your study of the Song of Solomon deepened your understanding of the ministry of Christ to his bride, the church?

How does the Song of Solomon's presentation of King Solomon enhance your understanding that Jesus Christ is "something greater than Solomon" (Matt. 12:42) as our Savior and King?

How has your study of the Song of Solomon furthered your understanding of the effect of the curse of Genesis 3:16 on the marriage relationship, and thus your understanding of how Christ is essential to a healthy marriage?

> ### Theological Soundings

How has the Song of Solomon deepened your appreciation of marriage as an institution designed by God to provide companionship, further the human race through the bearing of children, and show forth the mystery of Christ's relationship to his church?

How has the Song of Solomon impacted your understanding of the essential nature of male and female complementarity in the institution of marriage?

The Song of Solomon reveals that love is the "very flame of the LORD" (8:6). How have you grown in your understanding of human love through your study of the Song of Solomon?

In addition, how have you grown in your understanding of God's love through your study of the Song of Solomon?

We see in the Song of Solomon that marriage takes place in a larger social context. Family, friends, and society at large play a role in this book. How has your study of the Song of Solomon influenced your understanding of the importance of the wider community in choosing a spouse?

How has your study of the Song of Solomon influenced your understanding of the relationship between marriage and childbearing?

As You Finish Studying the Song of Solomon . . .

We rejoice with you as you finish studying the Song of Solomon! May this study become part of your Christian walk of faith, day by day and week by week throughout all your life. Now we would greatly encourage you to study the Word of God in an ongoing way. To help you as you continue your study of the Bible, we would encourage you to consider other books in the *Knowing the Bible* series, and to visit www.knowingthebibleseries.org.

Lastly, take a moment to look back through this study. Review the notes that you have written, and the things that you have highlighted or underlined. Reflect again on the key themes that the Lord has been teaching you about himself and about his Word. May these things become a treasure for you throughout your life—this we pray in the name of the Father, and the Son, and the Holy Spirit. Amen.

KNOWING THE BIBLE STUDY GUIDE SERIES

Experience the *Grace* of God in the *Word* of God, Book by Book

——— Series Volumes ———

- Genesis
- Exodus
- Leviticus
- Numbers
- Deuteronomy
- Joshua
- Judges
- Ruth and Esther
- 1–2 Samuel
- 1–2 Kings
- 1–2 Chronicles
- Ezra and Nehemiah
- Job
- Psalms
- Proverbs
- Ecclesiastes
- Song of Solomon

- Isaiah
- Jeremiah
- Lamentations, Habakkuk, and Zephaniah
- Ezekiel
- Daniel
- Hosea
- Joel, Amos, and Obadiah
- Jonah, Micah, and Nahum
- Haggai, Zechariah, and Malachi
- Matthew
- Mark
- Luke

- John
- Acts
- Romans
- 1 Corinthians
- 2 Corinthians
- Galatians
- Ephesians
- Philippians
- Colossians and Philemon
- 1–2 Thessalonians
- 1–2 Timothy and Titus
- Hebrews
- James
- 1–2 Peter and Jude
- 1–3 John
- Revelation

crossway.org/knowingthebible